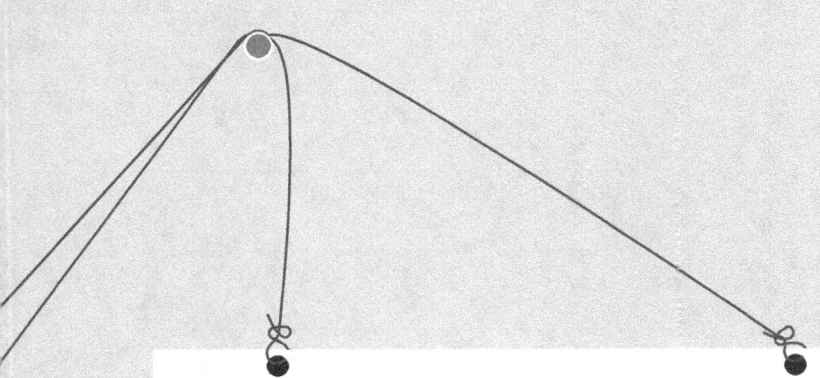

A MESSAGE FROM BABETTE

Mind Shifting Snippets are some of the best tips and inspirations I have come across during my 20 years of business consulting. They represent some of the deeper truths that I have learnt from my experience as an expert consultant in strategy and competition, and from the numerous clients I have been privileged to work with.

So whenever you find yourself at a loss for inspiration hopefully these snippets will help you break out of any bind you may find yourself in! They may also help you stretch your thinking.

Enjoy ...

Babette

He who does not contemplate the future is destined to be overwhelmed by it.

HG Wells

IDENTIFYING GROWTH

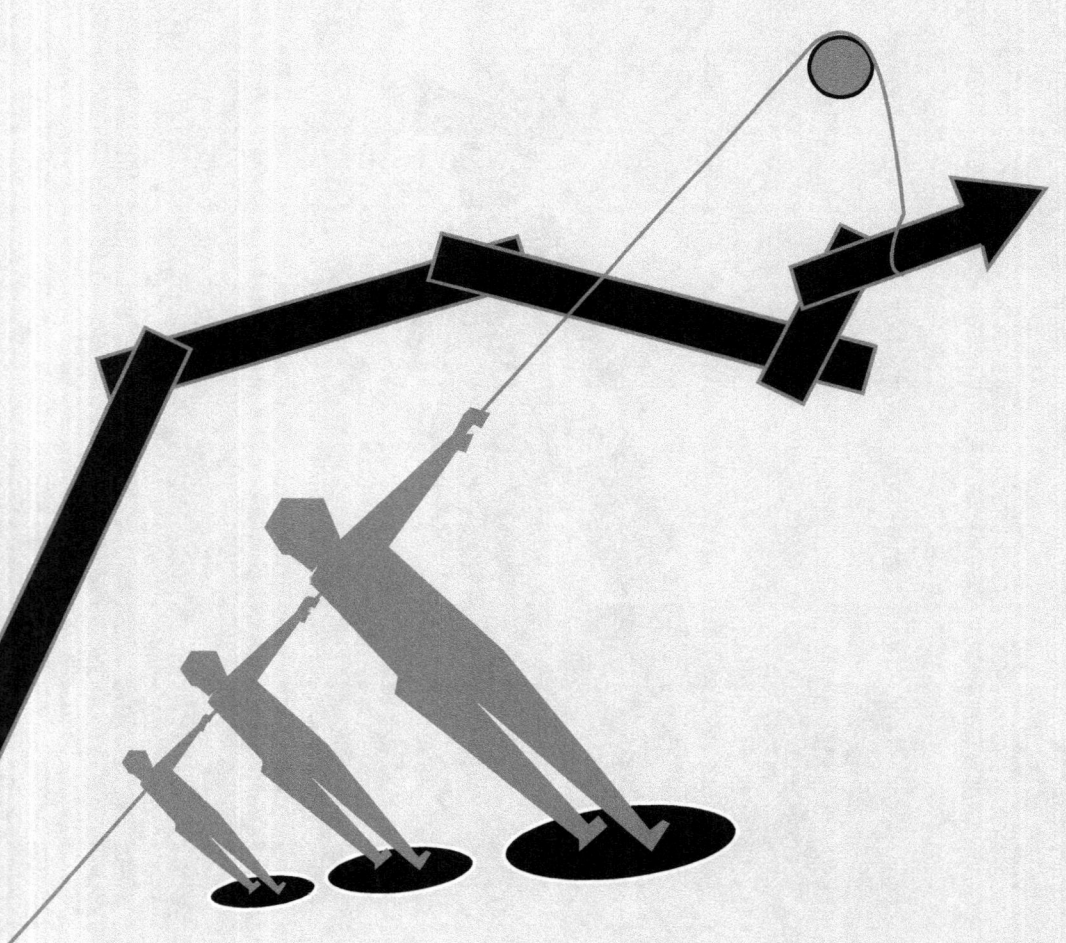

Companies that experience rapid growth have been found to use the future as their frame of reference rather than the present.

This is done by:

- Identifying a time in the future – usually five-ten years is long enough, however the exact point is not as important as a time frame that enables you to think away from your present constrictions. Tip: A point where you are able to say "anything is possible".

- Visualise and articulate what the business would ideally look like at that future point and include as much detail as possible.

- Reverse engineer your vision - question what it will take to make this vision a reality - determine what resources, skills etc. would be required.

- Plan the steps for each year needed to make this vision a reality. Factor in time frames and resources needed to reach your goal, and consider the competitive factors that may affect your success.

Use your vision and annual plans as a basis to effectively gather and analyse the competitive factors required to reach your goal – and adjust regularly to market forces, competitive challenges and opportunities as they arise.

As Walt Disney once said, "If you can dream it, you can do it".

PREVENTION & PROMOTION FOCUS

Do you think about your goals in terms of what you have to gain, or what you have to lose?

If your outlook is from the perspective of what you have to lose, this is termed **Prevention Focus**. Here the focus is on security, avoiding mistakes, and fulfilling responsibilities.

Promotion Focus is about looking at what you might gain, such as getting ahead, maximizing your potential and reaping the rewards. Research over the past decade shows that promotion focus leads to speed, creativity, innovation and embracing risk; while prevention focus leads to accuracy, careful deliberation, thoroughness and a strong preference for the devil you know.

Our greatest glory is not in never failing, but in rising every time we fall.

Confucius

In the current environment the focus for the majority of organisations is on security and not rocking the boat. However, without innovation and growth no business (and no job) will be safe for long. A new venture isn't a chance to get in front of the pack, it's a way not to fall behind.

If you have some great ideas for your organisation and wish your management was more comfortable with risk there are two possible solutions: either try and get them to adopt the promotions mindset (difficult in this climate), or use the right language to work with their prevention mindset instead, i.e. re-frame your great idea as an opportunity for avoiding loss, rather than making gain.

10 UNIVERSAL TRUTHS

Things to Know and Think About

1. Even under ideal conditions people have trouble locating their car keys, reading glasses or finding their mobile phone - but everyone can find and push the snooze button - eyes closed, first time, every time!

2. Bad decisions make great stories.

3. In every plate of chips, there is a bad chip.

4. Nothing is more frustrating than a moment during an argument when you realise you're wrong.

5. There is great need for a sarcasm font.

You never know when it will strike, but there comes a moment at work when you know that you just aren't going to do anything productive for the rest of the day.

6

Was learning cursive really necessary? How many documents or letters are you hand writing today?

7

There's no worse feeling than that millisecond you're sure you're going to die after leaning your chair back a little too far.

8

The only time you look forward to a red light is when you are trying to finish a text.

9

Sometimes you'll look down at your watch 3 consecutive times and still not know what time it is - welcome to shallow brain!!

10

10 TIPS ON MARKETING STRATEGIES

1   Be clear about the direction your business is going in.

2   Be close to your customer and know which products give the highest margins and why. Establish a database for your clientele.

3   Be certain of getting good repeat business and referrals - these are the cheapest forms of marketing.

4   Watch your opposition and see where they fail and where you can improve.

5   Look at your business from an outsider's perspective. Do products need to be improved or dropped?

Think of something imaginative and clever to use as the basis of a small, inexpensive advertising campaign in your local newspaper. 6

Learn how to do a SWOT analysis properly - strengths, weaknesses, opportunities and threats. 7

Eighty per cent of income is generated by 20 per cent of customers. Analyze how you can increase the income from this group. 8

If discounting, be careful with your cost structures. If you are going to advertise, set specific objectives - to who, why, and where and when, as well as what you will say and how you will say it. 9

Each day look for a new type of customer. Defining how to get that customer is the job of marketing. 10

Nothing is more difficult, and therefore more precious, than being able to decide.

Napoleon

GOOD DECISION-MAKING

Good decision-making is critical to good leadership, but there is a tendency to get stuck in a mindset or point of view - especially if the stakes are high. According to the Harvard Business Review, there are 3 common traps that decision-makers need to avoid:

Anchoring: even if the first information that you are given seems right - take the time to pursue other lines of thinking. Don't give a higher weighting to the first information that you are given.

Status Quo: ask yourself, does keeping the status quo really serve your needs or should you be exploring other options and opportunities?

Confirming evidence: try to avoid people who always agree with you. If you are finding that information constantly validates your existing point of view, review with a trusted colleague and ask them to argue against your perspective.

It's well worth the extra time involved to step through the above points before taking a final decision, and avoid some of the decision-making traps!

There is much pleasure to be gained from useless knowledge.

Bertrand Russell

APPLYING
KNOWLEDGE

What used to matter was your accumulated knowledge. What matters now is how quickly and efficiently can you find and use the information you need to solve a problem.

In a product-centric world, you could take the time needed to research. In a customer-centric world, you only get a minute to find the right information quickly. The competitiveness of your organisation increasingly depends on your ability to rapidly find and consolidate the information that's needed to take action.

Your company is like a jet fighter. The more quickly your people can put together the information they need to make good decisions, the more competitive you will be.

Change your thoughts and you change your world.

Norman Vincent Peale

AQUIRED KNOWLEDGE

Companies that focus on their unique abilities are best positioned for growth.

Ask the following three questions:

1   Why do our customers choose us over our competitors?

2   Which of our capabilities make us stand out against our competitors?

3   How difficult would it be for a start up company to replicate what we have done?

If you can determine your uniqueness, in fact your most crucial asset, then you have identified the focus of your growth.

Know your enemy, know yourself and your victory will not be threatened. Know the terrain, know the weather and your victory will be complete.

Sun-Tzu

VERIFYING INFORMATION

The internet has made researching deceptively easy. It's easy to find information, but if the accuracy of the information isn't verified, mistakes can be sent around the world with a single click.

In order to avoid this, keep the following guidelines in mind:

- Be wary of facts where no source is listed - electronically, in print or on TV. Check more than one source to validate facts.

- Attribute quotations correctly - check quotation accuracy with a reputable reference book.

- Avoid using an exceptional situation to prove a key point - you may be asked to provide further proof.

- Consider the context - if taken out of context you may set yourself up for embarrassment, the point being made by the recognized expert may be exactly the opposite.

- Consider the validity of other positions on an issue - to provide balanced and objective analysis of a subject.

Verifying your information will avoid the embarrassment of mistakes being brought to light by an audience, or published world-wide with a single click.

PROBLEM SOLVING

There are many elements to creative problem solving, including the ability to better analyse what you see.

Here are some tips to improve your creative ability and analysis:

| Take things apart and put them back together again - when you do this, could you have left parts out? What is the relationship between the parts?

| Look at a problem from differing points of view.

| Use your imagination to determine the order and steps required, and understand why this order and steps?

| Take notice of cycles or systems in the world - are they essential for things to function?

Sort things in different ways.

Look for double meanings and hidden elements (parallels to past prcblems)

Find "ing" words (gerunds): i.e. if you want to build a bicycle you would use the words: sitting, pedalling, steering, braking, leveraging etc. Use this concept with other problems.

Look at social trends and review what futurists are talking about.

Identify key analytical techniques that will provide you with appropriate insights.

Do you have a process to solve your problems creatively?

6STRATEGIES
for Avoiding Risk

Leaders need to be strategic to avoid putting their company at risk. While you concentrate on potholes, you'll miss windfall opportunities, and any signals that the road you're on is leading off a cliff!

Anticipate: most companies focus on what is directly ahead. Leaders require 'peripheral vision' - look for game-changing information, and build wide external networks to help you scan the horizon better.

Think Critically: reframe problems to understand the root causes, challenge current beliefs and mindsets, uncover hypocrisy, manipulation and bias.

Interpret: hold steady and synthesise information from many sources before developing a viewpoint.

Decide: develop processes and enforce them, so that you arrive at a "good enough" position.

Align: foster open dialogue, build trust and engage key stakeholders, especially when views diverge.

Learn: it is essential to get honest feedback - have rigorous debriefs, celebrate success and failures that provide insight, and shift course quickly if you are off track.

Adapted from: "6 Habits of True Strategic Thinkers",
http://www.inc.com, March 20, 2012

A common mistake that people make when trying to design something completely foolproof is to underestimate the ingenuity of fools.

Douglas Adams
Author of "Hitchhiker's Guide to the Galaxy"

IN
DENIAL

Denial is the unwillingness to acknowledge and deal with reality. The cost of denial for an organisation can be enormous.

Even the best leaders can be in denial about trouble inside the organisation, about competitor behaviour, about customer behaviour. Leaders need to become ruthlessly realistic in order to see the world as it is now, not how it has been previously or how they wish for it to be.

The example of General Motors describes an organisation with a dysfunctional business model for decades. Observers knew it, the company chose to ignore it. GM believed their past success would continue indefinitely. In 2008, they behaved as if it were still 1988 and paid the ultimate price - the firm went bankrupt.

Young companies are not immune to denial either. Consider the dot-com bubble... A flawed business model cannot be overcome by wishful thinking. How can organisations detect denial warning signs before it is too late? Often middle managers on the front line are exposed to the daily reality in the marketplace.

We do not deal with certainties. The world of intelligence is a world of probabilities. Getting the information is not usually the most difficult task. What is difficult is putting upon it the right interpretation. Analysis is everything.

Issur Harel
Former Head of Mossad

Companies have to encourage input, allowing managers and all employees to raise problems and to take action. Firms that deal with bad news badly e.g. by dismissing the person who bears that news, are not only in denial, they are sencing a message to employees that ensures future potential input will be silenced, cutting off that critical supply of market intelligence.

Consider your own company's behaviour - are you in denial or ruthlessly realistic?

Before you become too entranced with gorgeous gadgets and mesmerizing video displays, let me remind you that information is not knowledge, and wisdom is not foresight. Each grows out of the other, and we need them all.

Arthur C. Clarke

FACING
CHANGE

In the face of change, people tend to exhibit one of three characteristics - frightened, clueless or uninformed... If you want your organization to progress successfully you need to be able to identify and address the reasons behind these behaviours:

Uninformed people need the tools to gain the information and insight to go forward - they are not a major risk but need help to progress.

Clueless people not only don't know what to do but have no idea how to do it. They not only need to be advised how to go forward, but be given an understanding as to why.

Frightened People will resist any help that you can give them, and will blame anyone around them for the stress the change is causing. The worst kind of frightened person is one with power.

PS: The root of the fear is often *the fear of being wrong*. How about turning that around? How about considering the possible consequences or opportunities being wrong can offer?

RECESSION
OPPORTUNITIES

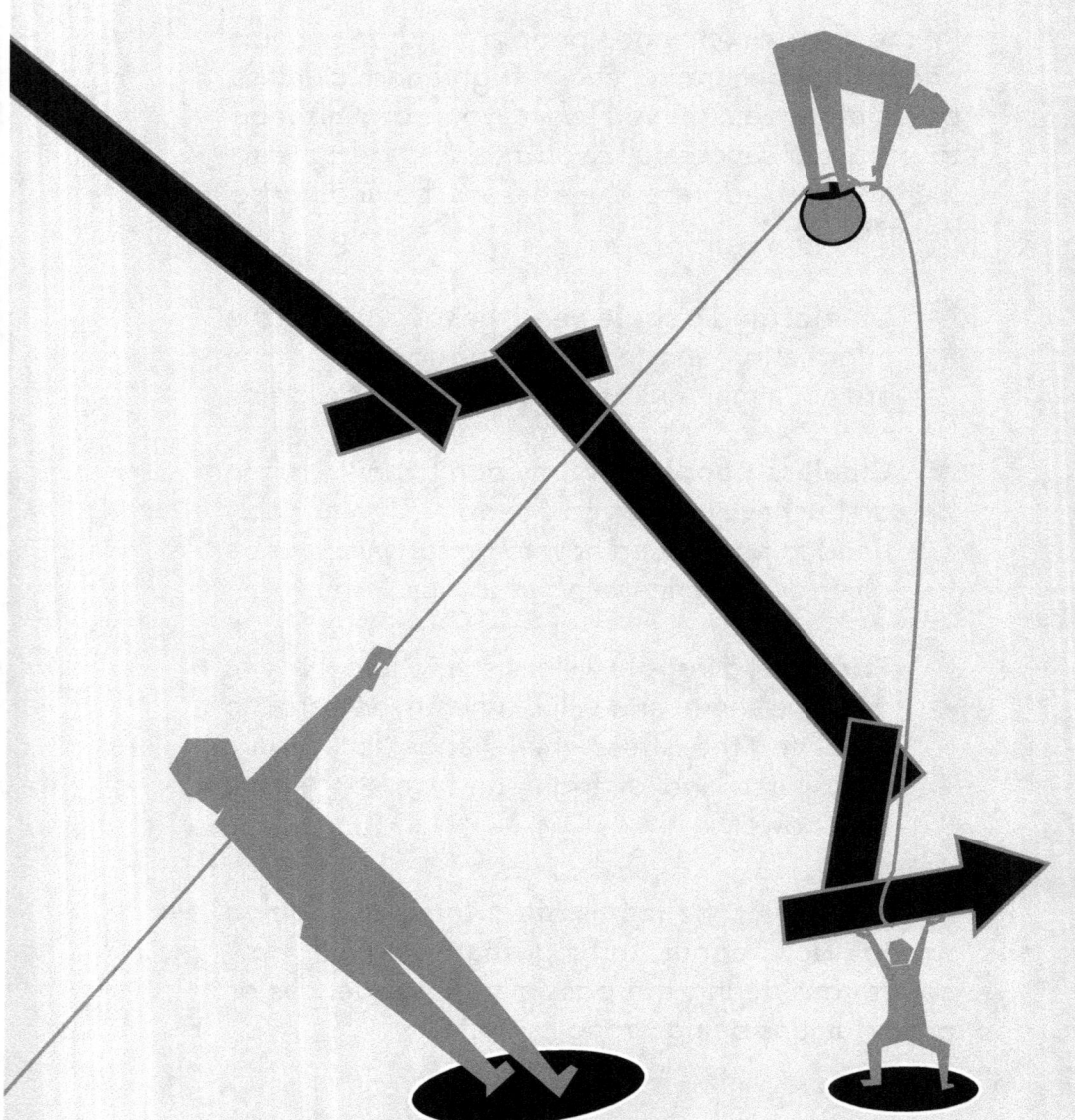

Recessions and economic downturns provide great opportunities if you emp oy the right strategies.

Firstly - don't panic! Stay focused, stay positive. What else should you do? Here are a few ideas:

Define your desired outcomes - focus everything on achieving your goals. Evaluate every opportunity and measure performance against your goals.

Be disciplined, decisive and take action. Strong leadership is essential, involve your team and create a positive corporate culture.

Create a clear business and marketing strategy and follow a detailed plan. Maximize strategic partnerships. Understand what your competitors are doing and do it better.

Maximise R&D and innovation to attract business away from competitors.

Maintain tight cost controls by eliminating unnecessary spending. Ensure you have the funds to finance your goals.

Failure is not a single, cataclysmic event. You don't fail overnight. Instead, failure is a few errors in judgement, repeated every day.

John Rohn
Motivational Speaker

Enhance your value proposition, loyalty and brand. Don't discount, it erodes profitability and competitiveness.

Maximise customer service. Understand and know your customers, work with them to reduce costs, improve their efficiencies and grow their revenues.

Maximise the performance of your people, through training, incentives, empowering them and ensuring the right person is in the right job.

Be prepared to change. Examine every aspect of your business and encourage participation to increase efficiencies. Empower everyone to find new and more effective ways to achieve results.

You may need to see your company through a new set of eyes....to achieve the outcomes you require - even in an economic downturn.

The Chinese use two brush strokes to write the word 'crisis'. One brush stroke stands for danger; the other for opportunity. In a crisis, be aware of the danger - but recognize the opportunity.

John F. Kennedy

ENJOYING A RECESSION

It's time to be upbeat about the recession or during any economic downturn!

A recession offers new opportunities – hard to believe – but it's true. This is the time to identify emerging opportunities and take stock of the competitive environment. Ask any marathon runner or Tour de France rider, it's where the course is hardest, on the uphill stages, that the lead changes hands. That's where we are now.

In fact, this is the time to start a business, or take that new challenge. If you have a solid business plan or strategy, getting it off it's feet in the hard times leaves you ready to take full advantage as the economy improves. It's also the best time to review competitors' strengths and weaknesses, and use these to your advantage.

How skillfully you manage now will determine your position in the competitive field.

Our tips:
- Re-evaluate your competitors
- Re-examine your strategies
- Re-analyse your markets and potential opportunities.

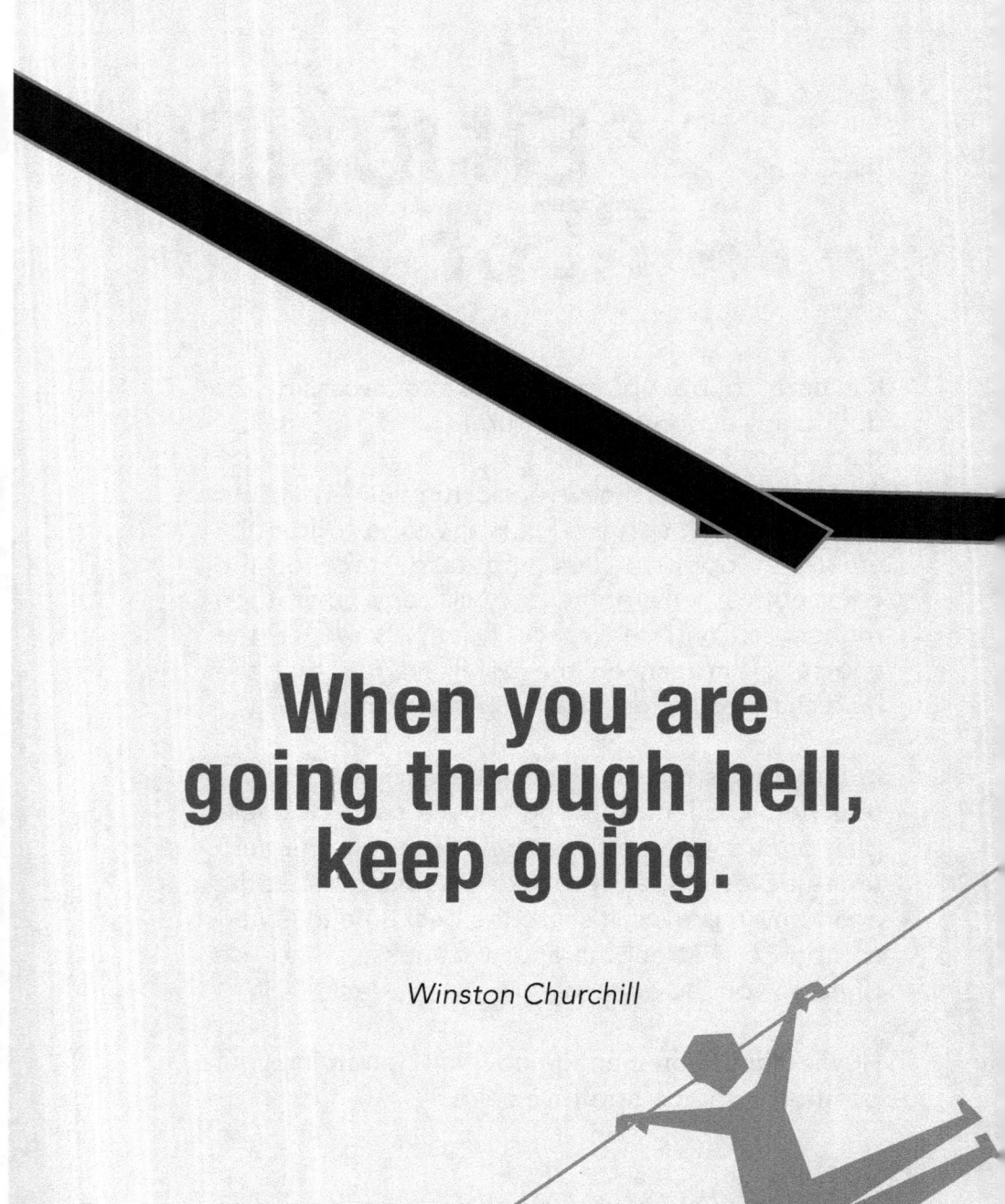

When you are going through hell, keep going.

Winston Churchill

5 TOP ISSUES
Keeping CEOs Awake at Night

1   Sourcing and retaining new staff, especially young talent. Employees are your biggest asset, so how do you build staff loyalty and retain them in the long term?

2   Achieving top-line growth. How can you grow sales, increase customer loyalty and sustain it ahead of competitors, all whilst maintaining costs?

3   Reducing costs in the current climate, especially wage and salary increases. What are the impacts of international trade, the GFC etc. on your ability to reduce costs?

4 Efficiency improvements - ensuring your strategies are appropriate for the business, and managing risks. Have you considered moving from existing tough ndustries e.g. retail, to a more profitable ore e.g. mining. Is it possible after weighing up the risks of diversification?

5 Managing increasing competition-competition is fierce and getting more intense. Are you equipped to recognise where growth opportunities are and respond quickly?

No doubt you are familiar with these issues too.

Strategy is about what your company wants to do with the world. Intelligence is what the world wants to do with your company.

Joseph Rodenberg

Managing Partner,
Rodenberg, Tillman & Assoc.

IDENTIFYING
TRENDS

Trends aren't fads. According to the Oxford Dictionary a trend is defined as "a general direction in which something is developing or changing." It defines a fad as "a craze, or a fussy like or dislike." Trends are long term, fads are temporary.

One of the important business skills to be developed over the coming decades is our skill in identifying trends, as opposed to fads.

Here are 6 tips for honing your trend watching skills:

1   Know why you're tracking trends

2   Don't get your trends mixed up (yes, some will contradict each other)

3   Know a fad when you see one

4   Don't apply all trends to all people

5   Be (very) curious

6   Benefit from the unprecedented abundance of information resources (think social media).

10 VALUABLE INSIGHTS
from the Guru Michael Porter

The following are 10 valuable insights from guru Michael Porter, many of which are highly unconventional!

1   The granddaddy of all mistakes is competing to be the best, going down the same path as everybody else and thinking that somehow you can achieve better results.

2   Confusing marketing with strategy.

3   Overestimating strengths.

4   Getting the definition of the business wrong or getting the geographic scope wrong.

5   The Worst Mistake: Not having a strategy at all.

6   Not addressing the hidden biases embedded in internal systems, organisational structures and decision-making processes.

7   Companies undermining their own strategies.

8   Strategy killers in the external environment.

9   If you listen to every customer and do what they want you to do, you can't have a strategy.

10   Single minded pursuit of shareholder value, measured over the short term, has been enormously destructive for strategy and value creation.

Nothing wrong with returning to basics - sometimes it's important to step back and take an outsiders view of your organisation.

What we see depends mainly on what we look for.

Sir John Lubbock

When you're finished changing, you're finished.

Benjamin Franklin

HARMFUL PRACTICES

In light of the current economic conditions, we thought we should point out three of the most common yet most harmful practices in decision-making that you should keep in mind.

1 Casual benchmarking

People tend to copy the most visible, and obvious business practices of a competitive organization without understanding the underlying purpose behind it. Few companies undertake the research and analysis to have a thorough understanding of the reasoning behind a strategy – is it the best strategy to improve your organisation's performance?

What would the possible downsides be?

And how could you do it more effectively?

2 Doing what has worked well in the past

Be careful to understand exactly why a strategy was successful previously. Is it relevant to the issue at hand, and is this strategy the best practice to resolve the current situation?

Be aware not to confuse success in spite of an action as opposed to success because of an action.

3   Following deeply held but unproven beliefs

This happens when management believes something will work or that it matches some assumptions that are held about what makes some organisations successful.

These assumptions or beliefs will resist change and affect judgements and choices, regardless of whether or not they are true.

Check whether your decisions are relying on intuition, personal or group beliefs or influencers who may have other agendas in play.

Avoiding these pitfalls can lead to competitive advantage and clear direction setting in the most difficult of times.

12 TRAITS OF A WEAK ORGANISATION

According to Seth Godin, by following these 12 traits you could bring an organisation to its knees.

1   Focus is on the urgent instead of the important

2   Use of vivid emotions and the visuals that go with them

3   Emphasis of noise over thoughtful analysis

4   Unwillingness to reverse course and change one's mind

5   Xenophobic and jingoistic reactions (fear of outsiders)

6   Defence of the status quo encouraged by an audience self-selected to be uniform

7 Things become important merely because others have decided they are important

8 Top down messaging encourages an echo chamber (agree with this edict or change the channel)

9 Ill-informed about history and this particular issue.

10 Confusing opinion with the truth

11 Revising facts to fit a point of view

12 Unwillingness to review past mistakes in light of history and use those to do better next time.

Is your organisation weak at the knees?

10 COMMANDMENTS
of Failing in Business

Follow these 10 commandments and your business will fail!

1 Quit taking risks. Once you're big and comfortable, settle in and avoid trying anything new.

2 Be inflexible. Truly inflexible people do more than fail to take risks. They are so set in their ways that they simply cannot see any other way of doing things.

3 Isolate yourself. There's nothing like a bubble to keep the riffraff away.

4 Assume infallibility. If something seems to be heading in the wrong direction, cover up – or better yet, wait till you have a full-blown crisis, then blame it on some external force.

5 Play the game close to the foul line. Don't bother asking "is it right?" Go straight to "is it legal?" which is only a short leap away from "can we get away with it?"

6   Don't take time to think. Charging ahead without thinking works. Just ask some lemmings.

7   Put all your faith in experts and outside consultants. They're expensive so they must be worth it, right?

8   Love your bureaucracy. To impede real progress make sure that admin concerns take precedence over all others.

9   Send mixed messages. Like the parent who tells the child: "Clean your plate or no dessert" but the kid gets his Tim Tam anyway. That'll work for bonus schemes, too.

10   Be afraid of the future. "Fear is that little dark room where negatives are developed," author Michael Pritchard once wrote. Go there and turn off the light.

Most people spend more time and energy going around problems than trying to solve them.

Henry Ford

I notice increasing reluctance on the part of executives to use judgment; they are coming to rely too much on research, and they use it as a drunkard uses a lamp post for support, rather than for illumination.

David Ogilvy

COMPETITIVE
THREATS

A survey of business executives on the topic of competitive threats came up with some surprising results.

What they found was that executives are in fact worried about a wider array of threats - not just from rivals. The competitive threats survey revealed that there is not one single list of concerns for corporations globally, but rather a series of lists that vary depending on the industry or region of the participants. However, one consistent concern across all industries is commoditisation. In fact, this is the single greatest threat, whether it comes from a competitor or from a disruptive technology.

The following implications are thought provoking:

Stockpiling cash may be making companies "dumb, fat, and happy"

The Healthcare response to commoditisation

Shifting social norms

Stockpiling cash may be making companies "dumb, fat, and happy"

With respect to maintaining competitiveness, there are two very different types of companies in today's markets, those that focus on innovation and change and those that remain highly cautious, sitting on cash, making very slow, very careful changes. These companies would rather sit on cash than move fast enough to remain market leaders. On the other hand there are few aggressive, highly creative Apples or Amazons that deliberately destroy their own products in an effort to force their teams to develop new options and innovations before the competition beats them to it. The cautious set of companies need to widen their competitive scope to seek early warning on companies that disrupt from outside their traditional circles and competitive sets.

The Healthcare response to commoditisation

In the world of biopharma, commoditisation comes in the form of mounting pressure from generic alternatives as patents expire, forcing dramatic pricing drops for the branded prescription medications. Drug companies are refining their pipelines to avoid me-too offerings, as well as offering highly targeted therapies. Pharmaceutical companies that hang onto the more traditional mentality will likely find themselves with ever-shrinking pipelines and become acquisition bait a few years from today.

The next best thing to knowing something is knowing where to find it.

Samuel Johnson

The greatest obstacle to discovery is not ignorance - it is the illusion of knowledge.

Daniel J. Boorstin
Historian

Shifting social norms

Social norms are connected to disruptions, which in turn are inter-connected to technological and economic shifts. Social norms have undertaken huge changes in recent years - note the impact of organisations such as Amazon (buying books), iTunes (music), Skype (communicating) and Facebook (socialising). Industries that thrive today could fall victim to different buying habits on the part of customers in the not-too-distant future. Companies that perceive this change today will be best positioned to adapt to it tomorrow.

What plans do you have in place to address the opportunity of commoditisation? Analysis of early warning indicators and blind spots can help open your eyes to many future possibilities.

Adapted from: "Competitve Threats", Fuld & Company WhitePaper, http://www.fuld.com, January 2012

ACCEPTING
FAILURE

Failure is one of the biggest indicators of future success in an entrepreneur. Many venture capitalists won't invest in a new enterprise if the founder has never undergone failure - why?

From failed efforts it is proven that we have our best learning experiences, we grow, and we gain the experiences necessary for future significant successes. The fact is that businesses will not assume the risks necessary for innovation and developments if they're not ok with the idea of failing on some level.

There are those who are so afraid of failing they will do anything to avoid it. The problem with fearing failure is that you ultimately avoid risk, and this can stunt your richest experiences. Apparently those who have never faced a failure in a product, division or business don't have the experience that is valued in business. However, no-one wants to fail!

We cling to our own point of view, as though everything depended on it. Yet our opinions have no permanence; like autumn and winter, they gradually pass away.

Chuang Tzu

The key is to manage for failures. Be prepared to share what went wrong and dissect it. Another strategy is to create a "disengagement process" for getting out of a project that is showing triggering signs of failure.

It could be assumed that it is simply less disappointing and easier to not work that hard and not reach success. The excuse is built in to the equation already. What would happen if you tried your hardest and it didn't work out? The real question is - what if you didn't? What could you be losing out on by never trying at all?

THE TROUBLE
WITH ARROGANCE

One of the biggest barriers to incumbents dealing with market transitions is *arrogance*.

Successful businesses are justifiably proud of their accomplishments, given that only about 40% of companies are able to celebrate their sixth birthday.

However, when confidence runs to arrogance, it can blind a company to the fact that the things that made it a great company, will not continue to make it a great company. Being a giant in today's industry doesn't guarantee even short-term success as industries collide and hungry start-ups around the globe keep developing innovating ways to siphon profits from even the most seemingly staid of industries.

The pace of change in today's world means that the job for every leadership team is to determine how they will manage the dual challenge of maximising the cash flow from today's business while investing to create tomorrow's businesses. Companies that wait too long will have swift and brutal retribution - just look at Kodak, Research in Motion and the Newspaper industry...

Only a handful of companies have demonstrated the ability to do this once; the set of companies that have done this several times is even smaller.

Arrogance is something we at MindShifts encounter regularly when facilitating strategy sessions and talking to incumbents. Strategic Planning facilitation by independent experts free from blind spots, politics and corporate arrogance is a powerful tool for an organisation.

Adapted from: "How Arrogance Can Blind Your Transformation Efforts", Scott Anthony, HBR Blog Network

**There are three
kinds of companies:
companies that try to lead
customers where they
don't want to go;
companies that listen
to customers and then
respond to their
articulated needs;
and companies that
lead customers where
they want to go but
don't know it yet.**

Gary Hamel

CUSTOMER SATISFACTION

To satisfy the customer is the mission and purpose of every business.

Whenever organizations are reviewing strategy, it's worth revisiting Peter Drucker's definition of business - a business is defined "by the want the customer satisfies when they buy a product or service."

Essentially, Drucker believed that the customer should be the focus of, and purpose for, the organization. He explained, "A company's primary responsibility is to serve its customers, to provide the goods or services which the company exists to produce. Profit is not the primary goal but rather an essential condition for the company's continued existence.

A business's ability to create and maintain customers is directly dependent upon its ability to produce innovative products and/or services. In order for a company to maintain and/or grow its market share, and deliver innovation, it must continue to out-think and out-produce its competitors not only in terms of the selection of products and services that it offers but also in terms of its pricing strategy and customer service.

Interestingly, the effective analysis of the competitive environment leads to better decision-making and customer service.

DEVELOPING
BUSINESSES

The key steps to developing a business effectively are:

▌ Determine the right target market and the segments within that market.

▌ Determine a strong value proposition for potential clients.

▌ Become familiar with the external landscape - threats, competition, new technology, economic and social factors.

▌ Don't try to create a market for your product or service-find an insatiable market and provide what they want.

▌ Make value your first priority and cost the second priority.

▌ Surround yourself with the right people.

Understand your market - don't try to sell them something they don't want.

Create a marketing plan to monitor progress. Research join ventures and strategic alliances.

Use new partnerships to leverage press coverage.

Stay focused and use available networking opportunities.

Many senior level executives-CEO, CFO, CMO, COO, believe that business development is an easy task they can take on in addition to their workload. Wonder how many of the above they can really manage? What are you doing effectively?

ONE
LINERS

The following top ten one-liners are some of the most memorable lines from the movies, and can be used to provide unforgettable advice that is simple, useful, and most importantly - fun!

"Houston,
we have a problem"
Apollo 13

"I'll be back"
Terminator

"I'm going to make him an offer he can't refuse"
The Godfather

"What we've got here is a failure to communicate"
Cool Hand Luke

"Carpe Diem, seize the day"
Dead Poets Society

"Go ahead, make my day"
Sudden Impact

"Life is like a box of chocolates, you never know what you're gonna get"
Forrest Gump

"We're on a mission from God"
Blues Brothers

"You talkin' to me?"
Taxi Driver

"Who you gonna call"
Ghostbusters

For hundreds of years,
one of the central planks
of a decent education
was being taught
how to find information.
In barely a half-dozen years, the
Internet has made
this skill all but obsolete.
Suddenly, it's sorting information
that's become crucial –
learning to identify flecks of
gold among the acres of bullshit.
Critical, skeptical, analytical
thinking has never
been more important.

SNAPSHOTS

The best information is not just in the "snapshots"..

When we seek information, what are we really reading, (or more likely skimming), to get the insights we need?

The web has become a giant highlights newsreel, and we have become adept at gaining information by skimming at high speed. When doing research on the web we often target the "snapshots" – the summary of a report, a synopsis of a book, the review of a film, highlights of key sports matches.

But real change is rarely caused by "snapshots". Real change with its accompanying feelings of discovery and satisfaction come from the detail that has preceded the climax. The highlights of a match are often a thrill due to the match play that has gone first. In reading reports, if only the summary is read, the valuable insights from within the detail of the report are lost. It is in the detail that the depth of information required to make sound decisions can be found.

So don't just speed read the "snapshots"...
the parts that you miss are there for a reason.

//

However beautiful the strategy, you should occasionally look at the results.

Winston Churchill

STRATEGIC
FACTORS

If you want a decent strategy, you need a firm grasp of reality, which means avoiding bad strategies. How do you define bad strategies?

According to Richard Rumelt, author of "Good Strategy Bad Strategy", they are characterised by one or more of the following factors:

- Fluff - defined as a form of gibberish masquerading as strategic concepts or arguments.

- Failure to face the challenge - if the challenge can't be defined, that particular quality of the strategy can't be assessed, and then improved or rejected.

- Mistaking goals for strategies - arguably this is the most common error.

- Bad strategic objectives - the challenge for senior executives is to set out subgoals that are both relevant and practical for the chosen strategy.

Make the above factors part of your strategic reviews and you may avoid some of the prevalent pitfalls!

The ultimate measure of a man is not where he stands in moments of comfort, but where he stands at times of challenge and controversy.

Martin Luther King

VALUE
OR PRICE

In a depressed economy, what are consumers looking for – value or price?

In the current market, contrary to popular opinion, people are looking for value. Value takes priority, as people can't afford to spend unwisely, or make the wrong purchase decision. Yet many executives focus on price.

In a depressed economy, you should aim to give more, improve quality and quantity, and bring confidence to customers' interactions. Rather than cutting prices and quality to increase market share, add value and increase the benefits of what you have to offer.

As the economy improves, you can take full advantage of a solid reputation and customer loyalty, over your competitors who focused on price.

Not everything that is faced can be changed, but nothing can be changed until it is faced.

Anon

MANAGEMENT
STYLE

Willingness to let go of and question ingrained beliefs is a huge competitive advantage in times of change.

We all have beliefs that we hold onto and which frame our decision making and management style. In times of stress we tend to hold onto these even tighter, and try and wrap ourselves in a secure blanket of an environment we understand.

In times of change, these ingrained beliefs need to be examined critically, and executives need to invite challenges and seek out contrary opinions. When entering unknown territory, we should be willing to ask the 'dumb' questions and be strong enough to question our most cherished ideas when a better one comes along. The executive who is willing to be challenged and listen to other points of view with an open mind, will be able to make far better decisions as they will be seeking to understand the wider picture. It's a difficult step for those executives who refuse to listen to the people they hired because they believe they know best.

Take the time to review your management style — do you really have all the answers?

Nothing is more difficult to undertake, more perilous to conduct, or more uncertain in its success than to take the lead in introducing a new order of things, for the innovator has for his enemies all those who are well off under the existing order of things, and only lukewarm defenders who may profit under the new.

Nicolo Machiavelli

BEING DIFFERENT

Strategy has been defined as "the creation of a unique and valuable position, involving a different set of activities," (Michael Porter, 1996). Yet most executives try to develop the capabilities that their fiercest competitors have already mastered. The concept of 'best practices' in fact, reveals a flawed mind-set. There are no universally superior methods that should be applied by ALL industry participants.

Such a model yields competitive convergence and the often destructive mode of pure cost-based competition. Instead capabilities should be nurtured with a clear focus on the company's desired differentiated position in the marketplace.

Where can you start? How about:

1　Innovation and product development

2　Customer service management

3　Operations planning and control

4　Purchasing, supplier, distribution development

5　Quality management

6　Attraction and development of people

Are your senior executives really developing a unique strategy or just playing catch up in preparation for price driven competition?

Your ability to learn faster than your competition is your only sustainable competitive advantage.

Arie De Gues

THE
COMPETITION

Companies that compete in head-to-head competition in today's overcrowded industries lead to a bloody "red ocean" of rivals fighting over a shrinking profit pool. While most companies compete within these red oceans, this strategy is increasingly unlikely to provide profitable growth in the future.

Tomorrow's leading companies will succeed not by battling competitors, but by creating "blue oceans" of uncontested market space ripe for growth. Can you determine if your ocean is red or blue? Consider the following questions outlined on the Blue Ocean Strategy website (www. blueoceanstrategy.com):

▌ Is your company facing heightened competition from domestic and international rivals?

▌ Do your sales representatives increasingly argue they need to offer deeper price discounts to make sales?

When the winds of change blow, some people build walls and others build windmills.

Chinese Proverb

Are you finding you need to advertise more to get noticed in the marketplace, yet the impact of each advertising dollar spent is falling?

Is your company focused more on cost cutting, quality control and brand management at the expense of growth, innovation and brand creation?

Do you blame your slow growth on your market?

Is commoditisation of offerings a frequent worry for your company?

List your key competitive factors, then list your competition's. Are they largely the same?

If your answer to most of these questions was 'yes', your company is stuck in a red ocean of bloody battles.

Are you thinking outside the box to make the competition irrelevant?

COMPETITIVE
ANALYSIS

Competing against a rival's strengths is a flawed strategy. Many companies choose to go after a competitor's core strengths instead of exploiting its vulnerabilities.

How can your organization determine how to attack competitors where they are weak?

Undertake these three forms of competitive analysis:

1 Competitor Analysis over and above the basic SWOT analysis. Use a model that will help company strategists assess a competitor's intent and objectives, and the strengths it is using to achieve them e.g. Michael Porter's Four-Corners Analysis. From there, you can identify a competitive strategy that plays to your company's capabilities.

2 Early Warning analysis that helps spot and assess industry trends and facilitates a discussion of future contingency plans. This is especially helpful in fast moving industries such as information technology and retail, where fast competitive execution is crucial.

3 Broad industry analysis techniques like scenario analysis that help spot relationships along a company's value chain that can aid competitive strategy.

Consider if your company's strategic focus is to emulate a rival's strengths or exploit it's weaknesses?

COMPETITIVE
ADVANTAGE

Contrary to accepted management guidelines – companies don't go in for complex analysis of moves and possible counter-moves of their competitors. In fact a McKinsey & Co survey of more that 1800 companies globally, found that companies are totally unprepared when a competitor strikes with a potentially damaging move.

Other key findings include:

▎ In spite of early warning techniques available, most executives learned about a competitive move too late to respond in time.

▎ A significant number of companies relied on intuition, (rather than the complex analysis extolled as best practice in management texts), and responded in a reflex manner to threats.

Competitive advantage can be gained from knowing which organisations will be slow to respond to a competitive challenge, or will be unlikely to change in response to a competitive move.

As experience shows, those companies who do take the time and effort to do the analysis of possible competitive moves and countermoves will always be several steps ahead of the game.

Greece is collapsing, the Iranians are getting aggressive, and Rome is in disarray. Welcome back to 430BC.

John Cleese

THE POWER OF PERSUASION

To influence is an art that has been lost in the volume of information that people are swamped with today.

One of the biggest hindrances to success is all about persuading the people you wish to influence. Even the best business proposal will not gain traction if you are unable to influence or persuade your target. The important thing is to influence and not just inform.

Following are five prongs of persuasion:

1 **Words**: Express yourself with positive, specific and precise words. Don't use negative, vague words.

2 **Rhetoric**: Use rhetoric to get your message across, include powerful messaging and use memorable phrasing.

3 **Emotion**: draw on emotions to get your message across. Create feelings such as pleasure, fear, safety, acceptance, and prestige. Decisions are based on emotions.

4 **Logic**: People need to justify their emotional decisions with reason. Help to interpret the facts, information and ideas that are available. Take a point of view. Lead others to draw *conclusions*.

5 **Trustworthiness**: demonstrate your integrity. People need to trust your personal values and genuineness before they'll believe or do what you say.

Information floods the airwaves, the Internet, and our in-boxes. And with that influx, influence has become rare. Yet channelled toward a goal, influence – not simply information – drives action and results.

A little knowledge that acts is worth infinitely more than much knowledge that is idle.

John Quincy Adams

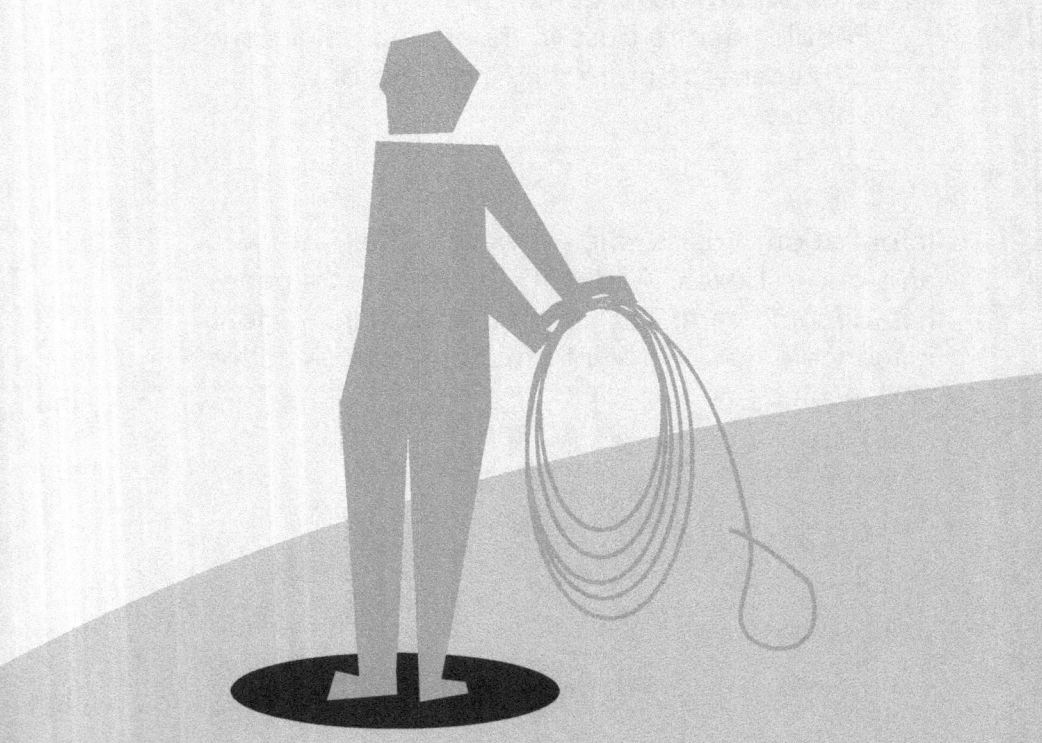

ABOUT MindShifts

The MindShifts Group is a world leading specialist in Competitive Intelligence (CI) and Strategy, helping major Australian and international corporations, in both public and private sectors, assess their CI needs, develop their infrastructure and capability, and deliver insights to key decision makers. Our experience and tailored services assist our clients to gain superior insights into competitors and the competitive forces they face.

With over 20 years in the field, MindShifts specialises today in providing advisory and consulting services, individual and group mentoring, war-games and facilitated workshops on strategy, business planning and CI.

We focus on supporting our clients' competitive intelligence and strategic endeavours ...delivering a smarter way to compete!

What makes us leaders in our field?

- Our client-centric values; we provide personalised service with a high degree of communication in order to understand the needs of our customers

- Our ethical commitment

- Our deep understanding of CI and our abil ty to apply it to our clients' businesses

- Our focus on providing valued competitive insights

- Our internationally recognised expertise in business analysis

- Our comprehensive service offerings

- Our excellent track record

- Our highly experienced people

- Quality of our work

Contact MindShifts today to use our skills and expertise to benefit your organisation! **www.mindshifts.com.au**